Maple Sugar Festivals
Tapping for Sap

Lisa Gabbert

The Rosen Publishing Group's
PowerKids Press ™
New York

To Julie—many thanks.

Published in 1999 by The Rosen Publishing Group, Inc.
29 East 21st Street, New York, NY 10010

First Edition

Book Design: Michael de Guzman

Photo Credits: pp. 4, 16 © Robert Winslow/Viesti Collection, Inc.; pp. 7, 19 © Frank Siteman/Viesti Collection, Inc.; p. 11 © Giraudon/Art Resource; p. 12 © Renaud Thomas/FPG International; p. 15 © Steve Myers/ International Stock; p. 20 © Al Clayton/International Stock.

Gabbert, Lisa.
    Maple sugar festivals: tapping for sap / by Lisa Gabbert.
        p.   cm. — (Festivals! USA)
    Includes index.
    Summary: Explains how maple syrup is made and describes some of the activities that mark sugaring season, such as parades, hay rides, and horse-drawn sleighs.
    ISBN 0-8239-5340-8
    1. Harvest festivals—New England—Juvenile literature. 2. Harvest festivals—United States—Juvenile literature. 3. Maple syrup—Juvenile literature. 4. Maple sugar—Juvenile literature.
[1. Harvest festivals. 2. Maple syrup. 3. Maple sugar. 4. Festivals.] I. Title. II. Series.
GT4405.G33 1998
394.26—dc21   98-17894
                                           CIP
                                           AC

Manufactured in the United States of America

Contents

Celebrating an American Tradition

People have been making maple syrup and maple sugar for hundreds of years. It is part of American **heritage** (HEHR-ih-tij). Towns and cities often celebrate this time with festivals. Some farms will have their own maple sugar festivals. These small farms are called sugarhouses, or **sugarshacks** (SHUG-er SHAKS). Sugarshacks welcome visitors during this time. Visitors can watch maple syrup being made. On weekends, breakfast is served at the festivals. That's when you can try their maple syrup!

Visitors to a sugarshack can see a bit of history as they watch the making of maple syrup.

Maple Sugar

Maple syrup and maple sugar are made from the **sap** (SAP) of maple trees. Sap is a watery, sweet liquid found inside a tree. Sap moves throughout the tree, and carries water and food to all the tree's different parts through tiny tubes inside the tree.

Some farmers grow maple trees so they can collect the sap. An area in the woods where maple trees grow is called a **sugarbush** (SHUG-er-bush).

Maple trees can be found in parks and backyards. There may even be one outside your house. ▷

The Maple Sugar Region

Maple sugar is made mostly in the northeastern part of the United States and in southeastern Canada. There, the winters are long and cold and maple trees grow well. Canada produces more maple sugar than any other country in the world. The American states that make maple sugar include New York, Vermont, Connecticut, New Hampshire, and Maine, as well as northern Wisconsin, Indiana, Pennsylvania, Maryland, Massachusetts, Ohio, and Michigan.

◀ *Maple sugar is made in areas of the United States where the winters are cold.*

Native American Technology

The making of maple sugar is a very old practice. In fact, Native Americans first discovered how to make maple sugar. Most tribes who lived in the cold, northern areas of the United States and Canada used a special **method** (METH-ud) of tapping trees for sap. They often used maple sugar for food, as gifts, or for trade. The Native Americans taught the art of maple sugaring to the early **colonists** (KOL-uh-nists).

Native Americans shared many of their practices with the colonists, including the making of maple sugar. ▶

Sugaring Time

Maple sugar is a kind of crop. Although most crops are **harvested** (HAR-ves-ted) in the fall, maple sugar is harvested in the late winter or early spring. During March or April, the **temperature** (TEMP-rah-cher) at night will sometimes drop below freezing, while the days grow warm. This rise and fall in temperature makes the sap run up and down inside the maple tree. When this happens, the sap is ready to be collected. This is called sugaring time.

◄ *At sugaring time, farmers will regularly collect sap that has been tapped.*

Tapping a Maple Tree

At sugaring time, maple sugar festivals are often held. Whether the festivals are in the city, a state park, or on a farm, **demonstrations** (deh-mun-STRAY-shunz) are the main event. First, a taphole is drilled into a maple tree. The taphole is not deep, so it doesn't hurt the tree. A **spile** (SPYL), or spout, is pushed into the hole and a bucket or plastic bag is hung from the spout. The sap from the tree drips through the spout and into the bucket.

During sugaring time, silver buckets hang from maple trees at many northeastern farms. ▷

Boiling the Sap

Boiling the sap is part of festival demonstrations. After the sap is collected, it is boiled. This removes water from the sap. While it boils, the sap must be **skimmed** (SKIMD) and watched carefully so that it doesn't burn. As the water **evaporates** (ee-VA-per-ayts), the sap turns into a dark brown, thick syrup. In order for this to happen, the temperature must reach 219 degrees Fahrenheit. Maple sugar is made when the maple syrup is left to boil some more.

Farmers have to be careful not to burn themselves while the sap is boiling. It can reach temperatures of over 200°.

Festivals of Heritage

Maple sugar festivals have more than just demonstrations. There are hayrides and rides on horse-drawn sleds. Street **vendors** (VEN-derz) sell food, and there is usually a parade through the town. Handmade crafts, such as quilts and sweaters, can be bought. There may also be a contest where one young woman wins the title of Maple Sugar Queen of the festival. After the Maple Sugar Queen is crowned, she rides in the parade.

Along with crafts and other maple sugar treats, the most popular item for sale at a maple ▷ sugar festival usually is maple syrup.

Maple Sugar Products

During sugaring time, many people eat food made with maple sugar. Many festivals serve pancakes covered in maple syrup all day. But there are other kinds of food as well. Maple cream, also called maple butter or maple spread, is syrup that has been boiled until it turns creamy. People also make maple jelly, mapled sweet potatoes, maple mousse, maple taffy, maple sugar candies, and maple ice cream.

◀ *Pancakes with maple syrup are just one treat that you can try at a maple sugar festival.*

Sugar-on-Snow

Making snow candy, or sugar-on-snow, is a fun way to eat maple syrup. It is one way Native Americans made candy long ago. First, syrup is boiled until it is thick. Then it is poured onto clean snow. The syrup turns waxy and chewy like taffy.

You can experience a part of American history by visiting a maple sugar festival. It's a time to celebrate an old technique and American history.

There may be a maple festival happening near you!

Vermont Maple Festival   St. Albans, VT
Pennsylvania Maple Festival   Meyersdale, PA

Glossary

colonist (KOL-uh-nist) A person who moves from his or her country to a new land, but stays under the rule of his or her own country.

demonstration (deh-mun-STRAY-shun) Showing people how to do something by acting it out.

evaporate (ee-VA-per-ayt) When a liquid turns into a gas.

harvest (HAR-vest) A season's gathered crop.

heritage (HEHR-ih-tij) The cultural traditions that are handed down from parent to child.

method (METH-ud) A specific way of doing something.

sap (SAP) The liquid inside a tree that carries food, water, and sugar to different parts of the tree.

skim (SKIM) To take something from the top of a liquid.

spile (SPYL) A tap or spout that is drilled into a maple tree.

sugarbush (SHUG-er-bush) The grove where maple trees are tapped and the sap is collected.

sugarshack (SHUG-er SHAK) A small maple sugar farm that welcomes visitors during the sugaring season.

temperature (TEMP-rah-cher) How hot or cold something is.

vendor (VEN-der) A person who sells things.

Index